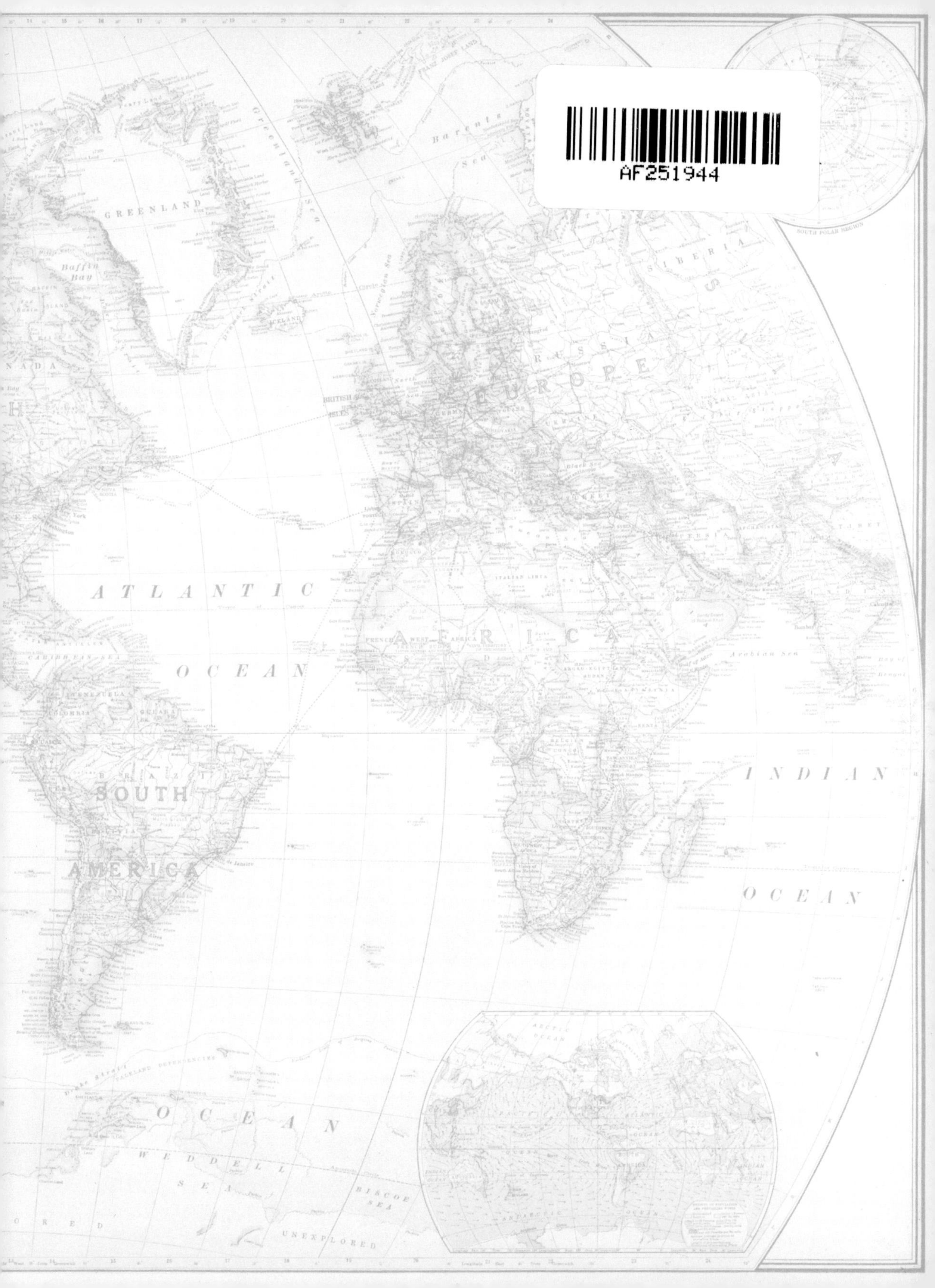

AF251944
GREENLAND
Baffin Bay
CANADA
ATLANTIC
OCEAN
SOUTH
AMERICA
OCEAN
WEDDELL SEA
BISCOE SEA
UNEXPLORED
EUROPE
RUSSIA
SIBERIA
AFRICA
FRENCH WEST AFRICA
Arabian Sea
INDIAN
OCEAN
SOUTH POLAR REGION
ARCTIC OCEAN

MY KIND OF COUNTRY
This journal belongs to
Keefe O'Brien
the Babe-magnet
El coolmo (Cumo)
KORN ACDC METALLICA

Expedition Journal

A Logbook for Travelers

LIST OF ILLUSTRATED PLATES

ADVENTURE PRESS

NATIONAL GEOGRAPHIC

WASHINGTON, D.C.

When I stepped off the airplane in Hartford, connecticut I was tired. then there were Johnathan & amanda who weren't tired at all & they wanted play with me, so I did. I jumped on the trampoline for a long time.

Now I am in Vermont. It is nice & wooded here. the B&B is really nice. the B&B is called ~~Country~~ Country Willows.

from maine Yesterday we drove to Burlington. It is very nice in Burlington.

Today we drove to Belfast, Maine. We had lobster for dinner. Maine has lots of forests. tomorrow we will raft.

Today we went river rafting. It was very fun. this guy fell off the boat 2 times. the rapids were just the right size. the guide was just like ted nugent.

P.S. Mom is a DORK!

Today we went to New York. I like New York. I like the tall buildings & all the people. My mom does not like it here. We went to the statue of liberty.

Now I am in Pennsylvania. we are in a haunted B & B. I am not scared at all. I had a good night sleep. No ghost problems at all. It was all just a lie to scare you. Most of the stories in the tomlineon guest book did not say anything about a ghost.

We went camping on cape Cod for 3 days. I got 7 bites on my back. Ow! the first night was Hell because it rained. the other 2 were fine.

The wedding was wierd.

Europe 7/2/06 – 7/26/06

1st night in Journeys Waterloo Hostel – London
hot, humid, no ventilation or A/C in room.

2 nights in Paris at Hotel Regina Opera.
TV - South Park in German
1st day walking around in late afternoon
+ evening after taking a looooong nap.

Hiram Bingham

"On all fours, we pulled ourselves up through the slippery grass, digging with fingers to keep from falling. Far below, the Urubamba snarled angrily."

— H.B.

OCCUPATIONS: Historian, archaeologist, and politician

GOAL: To search for the ancient cities of the Inca

ACCOMPLISHMENTS: Discovered several major Inca sites, including Machu Picchu; received the first National Geographic Society grant for archaeological research to fund his excavations of the site

AFTERMATH: Governor of Connecticut (1924) and U.S. Senator (1924–1933)

A Peruvian workman stands above the newly cleared ruins of Machu Picchu. Top: Expedition members pose before reed boats in the Peruvian port of Pacasmayo.

Hiram Bingham, a young history professor at Yale, had been to the Andes twice before when he mounted his own expedition in 1911. Somewhere in those towering highlands lay the ruins of the Inca capital, and Bingham was determined to find it. In the remote Urubamba Valley, Bingham learned of Inca ruins in the area and in a cold drizzle set out with a local guide. As the sun broke, Bingham found himself in a city of gleaming granite, tangled with jungle and wedged into a narrow saddle between two sugar-loaf peaks. Bingham christened the site Machu Picchu, after one of the peaks. A year later he was back with the manpower to liberate the sky-high city of granite from the jungle that had so long imprisoned it.

Eliza Scidmore

"Ceylon, in its natural beauties, is a fair pattern for Paradise, second only to Java— the most beautiful country on earth."

—E.S.

— OCCUPATION: Journalist

— PERSONAL GOALS: Reporting on foreign cultures and promoting international understanding

— ACCOMPLISHMENTS: Contributed 17 articles to NATIONAL GEOGRAPHIC and became the first woman on the Society's Board of Managers

— LEGACY: Expanded public awareness and appreciation of foreign cultures

Long before there were female anchorwomen, there was Eliza Ruhamah Scidmore. Though her first assignments were covering Washington, D.C.'s social scene, she knew party reporting was not for her. Taking to the road, she roamed Asia, reporting on ritual bathers at the sacred ghats of the Ganges, on tea pickers in Java, on Japanese prisoners-of-war, and on scores of other peoples and places in India, Java, Japan, China, and Ceylon (now Sri Lanka). By the turn of the century, her work was showing up in the pages of NATIONAL GEOGRAPHIC, and she soon became a foreign secretary for the Society and the first woman to serve on its Board of Managers. She spent her final years promoting the League of Nations.

Amelia Earhart

"That night I found over the Pacific
a night of stars.

They seemed to rise out of the sea
and hang outside my cockpit window,
near enough to touch,
until hours later
they slipped away
into the dawn."

— A.E.

OCCUPATION: Aviatrix

PERSONAL GOAL: To set world-aviation records

ACCOMPLISHMENTS: First woman to fly solo across the Atlantic; first aviator to fly solo from Hawaii to San Francisco

AFTERMATH: Her failed attempt to fly around the world and her disappearance over the Pacific made her a legend in aviation.

Earhart receives a congratulatory welcome in Oakland, California, after her 1935 flight from Hawaii. She began her love of the air as a passenger aboard a transatlantic flight in 1928 (above left).

Young, fearless, and elegant, Amelia Earhart gave up her job as a Boston teacher after a 1928 flight across the Atlantic—though the two aviators she flew with never let her touch the controls. In 1932, after soloing on her own record-breaking transatlantic flight, she became the glamorous but modest aviatrix, "the real American girl," out chasing sky-bound dreams few women had yet pursued. After setting records on transcontinental flights and on a flight from Hawaii, Earhart made her goal global: to circumnavigate the globe along the Equator. She and her navigator, Fred Noonan, made it to New Guinea, and on the morning of July 2, 1937, their Lockheed Electra took off from there, disappearing over the boundless Pacific. The real American girl was never seen again.

— BORN: Tutankhamen ca 1341 B.C., died 1323, served as king for nine years

— BORN: Howard Carter 1873, died 1939

— GOAL: To locate undiscovered tombs in the Valley of the Kings

— ACCOMPLISHMENTS: 1922 discovery of Tut's tomb, which renewed interest in Egyptian studies

— LEGACY: The discovery of Tut's tomb created a renewal in Egyptian studies that continues to this day.

A boy king dead some 3,300 years, a British archaeologist, and an English earl combined to create one of archaeology's most stunning discoveries. In the early 20th century, just as British scholarly interest in Egypt's Valley of the Kings was waning, Howard Carter began his search for the tomb of Tuthankhamun. So zealous was Carter's enthusiasm that he convinced Britain's Lord Carnarvon to back him financially as he searched the desert sands. Carter's ten-year search finally met with a spectacular conclusion, when in November 1922, he found the four largely intact rooms of Tut's tomb, filled with 5,000 objects. But his benefactor never saw the riches. Carnarvon died of an infection soon after the discovery, his death fueling the legend of the "pharaoh's curse."

Howard Carter and King Tut

"Mystery hung as heavy on the place as mystery ever can in the full light of day."

— Maynard Owen Williams
Writer, National Geographic

Left: The excavation camp in 1923. Carter's team (above left, Carter hatless) catalogued the most complete pharaonic tomb in history, which included a mummy similar to the one below.

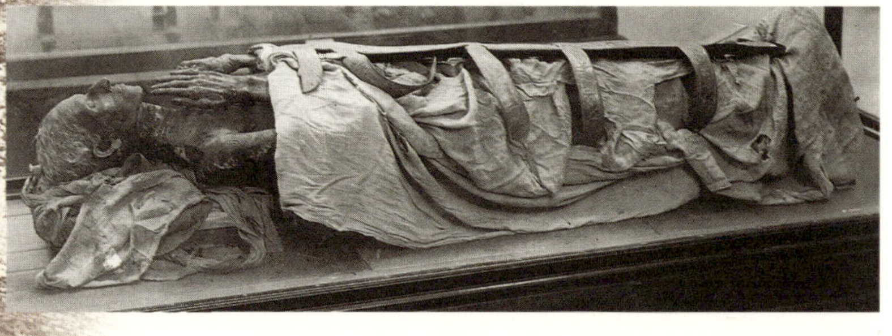

Robert Peary

"We are ready now for the final lap....

It is the time for which I have intentionally kept in the extreme rear.

From here on I shall take my proper place in the lead."

— R.P.

OCCUPATION: Engineer and Arctic explorer

PERSONAL GOAL: To be the first to reach the North Pole

ACCOMPLISHMENTS: Led seven expeditions to the Far North; led the first team to claim the North Pole in 1909

AFTERMATH: Despite the controversy surrounding Peary's claim to the Pole, his persistence encouraged successive explorers to venture to the Far North.

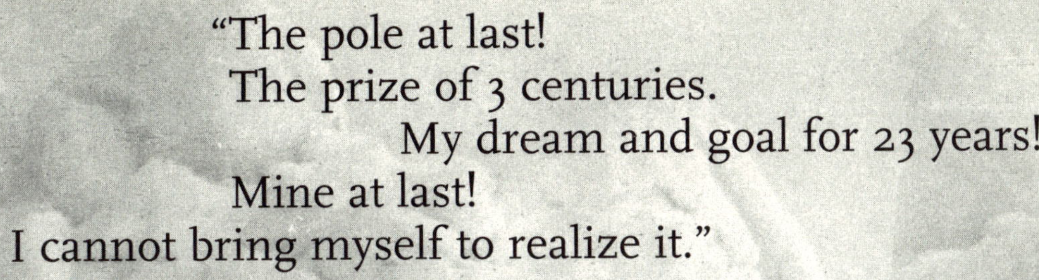

Above: Sleds and Inuit clothing were essential to the expedition's survival. Left: Matthew Henson was a key member of several Peary expeditions. Far left: Members of the 1909 party work beside their staked claim on the North Pole.

Even as a young man, Robert Peary yearned for fame, and daring schemes seemed the way to achieve it. In the decade around the turn of the 20th century, he ventured to the Arctic six times, attempting to set records in the "Farthest North" race. All of his attempts failed, but at age 52, he made a final try. On March 1, 1909, he set out with 23 men, 19 sledges, and 133 dogs.

Battling blizzards and open-water leads in the polar cap, the men pushed on. On April 6 Peary took a final observation and announced triumphantly that they had gained the Pole. In fact, they had gotten within five miles of it. Though Peary's ultimate claim to the North Pole has been mired in controversy, his adventures getting there rank among the world's greatest.

— OCCUPATION: Biologist, museum director

— PERSONAL GOAL: To explore and study natural history worldwide

— ACCOMPLISHMENTS: Discovered several new species of dinosaurs and found the first dinosaur eggs; explored the remote Gobi Desert; and served as director of the American Museum of Natural History

— LEGACY: Increased body of knowledge on dinosaurs

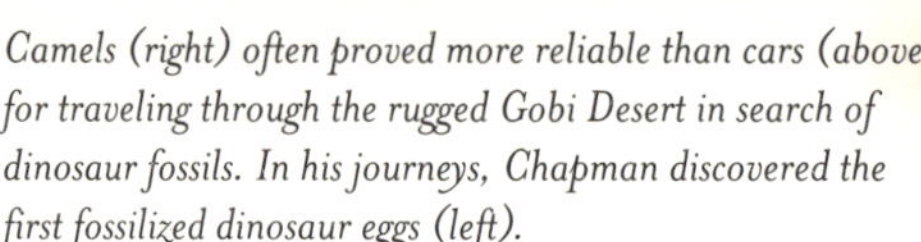

Camels (right) often proved more reliable than cars (above) for traveling through the rugged Gobi Desert in search of dinosaur fossils. In his journeys, Chapman discovered the first fossilized dinosaur eggs (left).

"For 25 years
I haven't stayed 12 months
in any one country. My home has been
wherever I make my campfire."

— R.C.A

Roy Chapman Andrews began his career cleaning floors at New York's American Museum of Natural History. He ended it as the museum's director. But the years in between were spent far from Manhattan. First studying whales in Pacific waters, Andrews then turned inland, spending an 18-month "honeymoon" collecting animal specimens in China, Tibet, and Burma. As a naval intelligence officer in World War I, Chapman got his first taste of Mongolia, a place that would prove to be a lifetime passion. Between 1922 and 1930 Chapman led car- and camel-borne scientific expeditions into Mongolia's remote Gobi Desert, where he uncovered a wealth of dinosaur fossils and the first cache of dinosaur eggs ever known to science.

"In the first fifteen years of field work I can remember just ten times when I had really narrow escapes from death. Two were from drowning in typhoons, one was when our boat was charged by a wounded whale; once my wife and I were nearly eaten by wild dogs, once we were in great danger from fanatical lama priests; two were close calls when I fell over cliffs; once I was nearly caught by a huge python, and twice I might have been killed by bandits." —R.C.A.

Roy Chapman Andrews

"When we turned in the first night,

Valley of 10,000 Smokes

"Avalanches of ashes on the neighboring hills could be heard,

and these sent forth clouds of suffocating dust and ashes.

—R.F.G.

EXPEDITION MEMBERS: Robert F. Griggs led B. B. Fulton and L. G. Folsom in 1915, and a contingent of 19 scientists in 1919.

GOAL: To study the effects of the 1912 eruption of Alaska's Mount Katmai

ACCOMPLISHMENTS: Mapped the extent of volcanic ash fall in the Valley of 10,000 Smokes

LEGACY: Expedition's findings led to the establishment of Katmai National Monument in 1918, becoming a national park in 1980.

we were astonished to find
that the ground under our tent was decidedly warm.
On examination we found
that a thermometer thrust 6 inches
into the ground promptly rose
to the boiling point."

—ROBERT F. GRIGGS
Expedition Leader

Members of the 1919 expedition peer over the rim of
Mount Katmai (far left), whose 1912 eruption left hundreds
of smoking fumaroles (above), and tossed ash for hundreds of
miles. A spring tunnels under a dust-covered snowbank (left).

When Mount Katmai erupted on the Alaska
Peninsula in June 1912, it was called "one of
the most tremendous volcanic explosions ever
recorded." In its wake it left a lunar-like landscape
pocked with steaming fumaroles. It was into that
remote Valley of 10,000 Smokes that a National
Geographic expedition under Robert F. Griggs
ventured briefly in 1915. So impressed were the
expedition members with what they saw that they
returned four times in the next four years to study
the geology and natural history of the remote,
difficult-to-reach valley. Braving bears, lack of
supplies, sandstorms, and ash slides, they none-
theless did groundbreaking work on how the
Earth heals itself after devastation.

EXPEDITION MEMBERS: Lt. Comdr. Zachary Lansdowne and a crew of 38 others

DIMENSIONS: 682 feet long, 2,115,000-cubic-foot capacity, top speed 60 mph

GOAL: To prove the efficacy of rigid airship design

ACCOMPLISHMENTS: Toured 9,000 miles along American coasts and interior, generated positive publicity for airship technology

AFTERMATH: Destroyed in a storm over Ohio in 1925

"The cruise of the *Shenandoah* was over an uncharted world.

Beacons by sea and signs by land
have been built through the ages for those
who voyage on the surface." —JUNIUS B. WOOD
Expedition Member

The 1924 tour of the U.S. brought the Shenandoah
to many cities, including Washington, D.C. (above).
Baskets were needed to lift men and supplies to the dirigible
(far right). It crashed in a 1925 storm (right).

Airship USS *Shenandoah*

On a dawn morning in October 1924, the U.S. Navy pulled its latest marvel out of a hangar in Lakehurst, New Jersey. This particular technological wonder needed the sun's warmth to work. Pride of the fleet, the USS *Shenandoah* was a 682-foot-long airship, and the sun's help was needed to heat and expand the helium inside. Forty men were onboard as she set sail that day on a record-breaking 9,000-mile, 19-day flight back and forth across the continent. At stops along the way, the airship was tethered to mooring masts and her crew disembarked in basket elevators. An experimental flight to test the airship for both defense and commercial uses, the *Shenandoah's* long voyage also entertained admiring Americans, who gathered to watch the Navy's streamlined lady put into port.

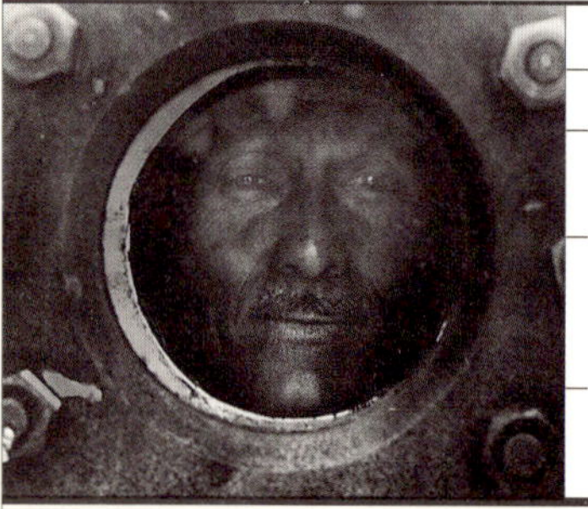

— OCCUPATION: Zoologist

— PERSONAL GOAL: To invent a submersible that would allow humans to explore the underwater world

— ACCOMPLISHMENTS: Officer of the New York Zoological Society 1899–1961; co-inventor with Otis Barton of the bathysphere diving mechanism, reaching a final depth of 3,028 feet off the coast of Bermuda in 1934

— LEGACY: Paved the way for Jacques Piccard's 1960 bathyscaph and other cutting-edge submersibles

William Beebe

From the bathysphere portal, Beebe peers out at the underwater world (far left). Radio contact had to be constantly maintained with the surface (above left). Beebe opens the water-filled submersible after an unsuccessful test (above).

When William Beebe crawled into his steel bathysphere in 1930 and descended a quarter-mile into the ocean off Bermuda, he may as well have been flying to the moon. It was before the age of the Aqua-Lung, and humans couldn't venture far below the surface with the diving gear then available. But Beebe was determined to develop a small submersible to take him into the depths.

And with the help of engineer Otis Barton, he did. Looking through the small quartz portholes of the bathysphere, he and Barton peered into "a world wholly new to human eyes, as strange as a Martian landscape." In the four years following that first dive, Beebe braved greater depths, finally descending 3,028 feet and blazing a watery trail for other underwater explorers to follow.

The Leakeys

"In Africa, survival depends on your reaction to irregularities
in your surroundings.

A torn leaf, a paw print,
a bush that rustles when there is no breeze,
a sudden quiet—
these are the signals that spell
the difference between life and death.

The same instant recognition of something different...
leads to the discovery of fossils." —L.S.B.L.

BORN: Louis S. B. Leakey (1903–1972), Mary Leakey (1913–1996),
Richard Leakey (1944–)

GOALS: To find fossils of our early man ancestors

ACCOMPLISHMENTS: Found fossils of early man including *Australopithecus boise*
(1959), *Homo habilis* (1960), *Homo erectus* (1984, with Kamoya Kimeu), and
the 3.6-million-year-old footprints of a hominid group at Laetoli (1978);
Richard is now a major force in African wildlife preservation.

LEGACY: Focused attention on Africa as the evolutionary cradle of humankind

In a lifetime spent scouring the parched gorges of East Africa, Louis and Mary Leakey found the buried treasure they were searching for. Not the riches coveted by most treasure hunters but the skulls, bones, and scattered fossilized remnants of humankind's distant ancestors. The skulls they uncovered in mid-century reordered the world's thinking on human evolution. But besides his contributions to our understanding of early man, Louis gave primatologists Jane Goodall and Dian Fossey their start, sending them into the field to study man's closest relatives—the apes. The Leakeys' son Richard has continued where his parents left off, discovering fossils that push man's ancestry far back into prehistory, as well as championing African wildlife conservation.

"I have lived on excitement
for the last ten years
and a humdrum existence
is next to unbearable to me."

— J.R.

Joseph Rock

"The king's uncle, a dried mummy, plastered and gilded,

sat in a golden chorten (shrine) in the same room

where we had lunch." —J.R.

OCCUPATION: Botanist and journalist

PERSONAL GOAL: To document the native flora and cultures of central Asia

ACCOMPLISHMENTS: Wrote about his travels across Asia in ten articles for NATIONAL GEOGRAPHIC; sent 60,000 botanical specimens back to the U.S.

LEGACY: Increased Western awareness of the natural history and cultures of Asia

Lama priests perform a ceremony in Muli, in today's Sichuan (left). The four-year-old High Lama of Yongning sits enthroned (above left). Rock's travels acquainted him with the tribespeople of Assam's Himalaya foothills (above) and took him to western China's Yalong River (above center).

Austrian-born Joseph Rock spent a sickly but brilliant childhood in Vienna, teaching himself Chinese but disdaining formal education. Despite his lack of schooling, he became a noted linguist, artist, photographer, and botanist. His searching intellect and wandering feet led him across Europe, North Africa, and North America. But Asia was his great love. Early in this century, he braved its brigand-infested hinterlands, exploring, botanizing, and writing and photographing for NATIONAL GEOGRAPHIC. His expeditions included entourages of servants, soldiers, and porters. Though often autocratic, Rock is still fondly remembered by older Chinese villagers as "Luo Boshi," the eccentric foreigner who lived among them and helped them in times of need.

"We had pierced the veneer of outside things.

We had suffered, starved and triumphed."

—FRANK HURLEY
Endurance *Photographer*

— OCCUPATION: Explorer and expedition leader

— EXPEDITION MEMBERS: 28 men in addition to Shackleton

— GOAL: To cross the Antarctic continent

— ACCOMPLISHMENTS: Though the expedition failed in its goal, it succeeded
in a herculean effort to rescue the men of the expedition.

— AFTERMATH: Shackleton died on a return journey to South Georgia Island,
and is buried there.

Ernest Shackleton

With Endurance *trapped in Antarctic ice, a crewman gazes across the frozen Weddell Sea (above). As winter came, leads through the ice (far left) became scarce, and the men huddled around the ship's ever burning coal fire (top left), a substitute for the vanished sun.*

In the annals of exploration, Shackleton stands out as the man whose heroic success was based on failure. He had been to Antarctica twice before when he mounted a 1914 expedition to traverse the Great White Continent. When his ship, *Endurance,* became locked in pack ice and crushed, he and his 28 men found themselves floating at sea on the pack, at the mercy of winds, currents, and melting ice. Despite the desperate situation, Shackleton remained the consummate leader, and, miraculously, the group managed to sail in open boats to uninhabited Elephant Island. From there Shackleton and five others sailed another 800 miles to inhabited South Georgia. In the end, not a single man from *Endurance* was lost, and Shackleton's own endurance became the stuff of legend.

date   location

OCCUPATION: Naval officer

EXPEDITION MEMBERS: Forty-two scientists, fliers, and dog mushers wintered at "Little America."

GOALS: To do scientific research on Antarctica and make aerial survey of the South Pole

ACCOMPLISHMENTS: Successful flight to Pole and survey of 150,000 square miles of Antarctica

LEGACY: Established American presence in Antarctica

One of four expedition planes is unloaded from Byrd's bark, the City of New York (far left). Limitless ice of Antarctica glints in the sun below Byrd's plane (left), after months of winter darkness spent before the flight at the base camp (below).

Byrd's South Pole Flight

"We felt the lure of entering the unknown.
We got a kick, as we did many times thereafter,
by looking through our glasses
to spot something new
to put on our maps."

—RICHARD BYRD

The Great White Continent loomed large in the imagination of early 20th-century explorers. Roald Amundsen had planted the Norwegian flag at the South Pole in 1911, so American Rear Adm. Richard Byrd determined he would tackle the Pole by air. In August, his expeditionary force sailed south, four planes aboard their bark. Reaching Antarctica, they spent the next year doing scientific research and preparing for the polar flight. On the morning of November 28, 1928, Byrd and three others took off. Climbing the massive mountains of the Antarctic interior, they had to dump supplies to conserve fuel and gain altitude. Still, within a day, they had flown across the Pole, the first Americans to leave their imprint at the bottom of the Earth.

"The length of time
during which this ancient city flourished
would make the oldest cities of the United States
seem youthful."

—M.S.

Matthew Stirling
and the Olmec

OCCUPATION: Archaeologist

GOAL: To identify and describe the makers of colossal ancient basalt heads in Mexico's Tabasco and Veracruz regions

ACCOMPLISHMENTS: Made the first archaeological studies of the ancient Olmecs; on the staff of Smithsonian's Museum of Natural History for 30 years; served on National Geographic's Committee for Research and Exploration 1960–1975

LEGACY: Ongoing archaeological investigations of the Olmec, precursors to the Maya

"The ticks are not bad, are they?" I asked hopefully,

"No," said the driver, beaming. "When full like grapes they fall off....

There are millions of them, however." — M.S.

Unplowable mounds of earth had humped the fields and palm breaks of southeastern Mexico for as long as locals could remember when archaeologist Matthew Stirling and his small team arrived on the scene in 1939. Armed with the picture of an incised, pre-Columbian head taken by an earlier archaeologist to the area, Stirling began excavating the mounds. Plagued by ticks, mosquitoes, and heat, he and his teams returned several times in the years to come, unearthing more and more remains of the once great Olmec civilization: Stelae, carved stone altars, and massive but mystifying stone heads that were the signature of these mystifying and sophisticated people. Stirling's work established the Olmec as the *cultura madre* of Mesoamerica, predating even the mighty Maya.

En route to the Oubangui River, in today's Congo, and ultimately to the Indian Ocean, the Trans-Africa Expedition passed through Zinder, in today's Niger (right). Along the way locals helped the Citroëns negotiate marshlands (below) and proudly displayed customs like lip beautification (far right).

Citroën Trans-Africa

EXPEDITION MEMBERS: Georges-Marie Haardt, expedition leader, plus eight specialists and ten mechanics

GOAL: To explore the breadth of Africa and identify possible rail routes through French colonial Africa

ACCOMPLISHMENTS: Traveled 15,000 miles across Africa in nine months, from the northwestern Sahara to the East African coast and to Madagascar

AFTERMATH: Trans-Asia Citroën Expedition traveled across Asia from April 4, 1931 to February 12, 1932.

"Our original purpose was to demonstrate the feasibility of
motor transport...to trace a route which might later...

connect two of its greatest provinces,
now separated by thousands of miles of
desert and jungle." — GEORGES-MARIE HAARDT
Expedition Leader

Expedition

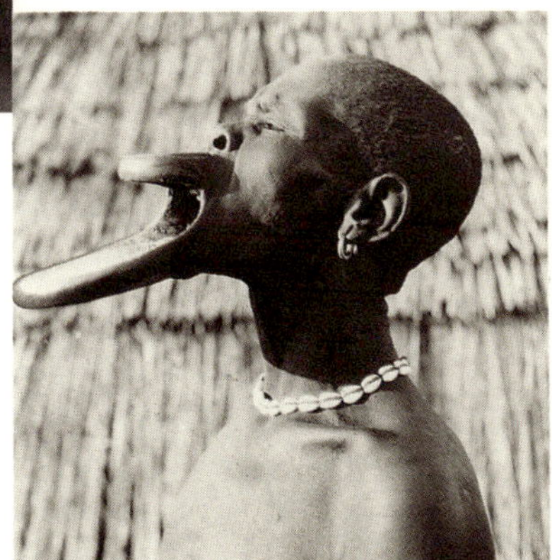

Even today, a 15,000-mile car trip from Algeria to East Africa would be an adventure, but in 1925 it was worthy of an expedition: the Central African Expedition "to demonstrate the feasibility of motor transport in these wild regions." The transports were actually eight ten-horsepower Citroën cars, each pulling a trailer and outfitted with a rear-end caterpillar system. For nine months the 17-member team motored through Africa, plowing through Sahara sands, African bush, and dense jungle; fording rivers; meeting sorcerers; and relaying messages by signal drum. But in the best bwana style they made it, bringing themselves and their Citroën caterpillars through Africa's "wild regions."

"We were now floating in the nearest approach

to a natural vacuum in which man has ever placed himself."

— ALBERT W. STEVENS
Expedition Leader

Explorer Balloon Flights

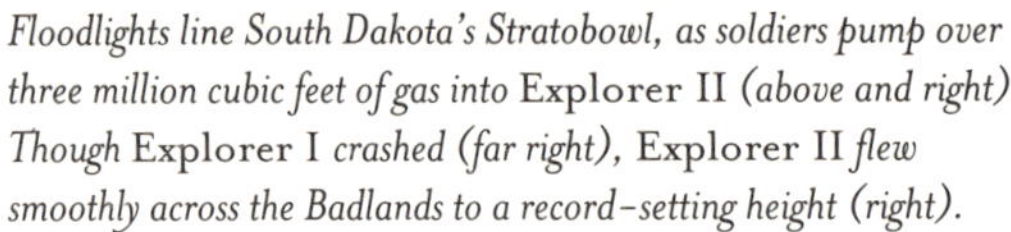

Floodlights line South Dakota's Stratobowl, as soldiers pump over three million cubic feet of gas into Explorer II *(above and right). Though* Explorer I *crashed (far right),* Explorer II *flew smoothly across the Badlands to a record–setting height (right).*

— EXPEDITION MEMBERS: Capt. Albert W. Stevens (leader, 1934 and 1935), Capt. Orvil A. Anderson (1934 and 1935), and Maj. William E. Kepner (1934)

— GOAL: To set a high-altitude record in aviation

— ACCOMPLISHMENTS: Reached a stratospheric altitude of 72,395 feet (13–71 miles)

— DIMENSIONS: *Explorer II* balloon 315 feet tall, 192 feet in diameter, capacity 3,700,000 cubic feet, gondola carried 3,000 pounds of lead weight ballast

— LEGACY: *Explorer II* altitude record stood for over 21 years.

"Suddenly and without warning
there came a great rent in our balloon!
A glance above us just a few minutes
before and all had been well;
soon we were dropping—
bag, gondola, instruments, and men."

—A.W.S.

"To look back, we were indeed in a strange predicament," Capt. Albert Stevens wrote in hindsight. He and two colleagues had been gliding through the stratosphere, 11.5 miles above the Earth, in their balloon, *Explorer I*, when the balloon ripped. As the rip widened, the men knew they had to abandon ship but were reluctant to. Finally, at 5,000 feet, one of them jumped, as the balloon exploded and the gondola plummeted through the air. The two other men had to force their way out, but all three parachuted to safety. The next year they were back in the stratosphere in *Explorer II*, this time reaching 72,395 feet without mishap, an altitude record that would stand for 21 years.

Jacques-Yves Cousteau

Over several decades of undersea exploration, Jacques Cousteau invented the Aqua-Lung (above) and the Diving Saucer (right), allowing humans to join sea turtles (above right) and other marine life in the submarine realms.

> *"If we didn't die,*
> *we would not appreciate*
> *life as we do."*
> —J.C.

OCCUPATION: Oceanographer

PERSONAL GOAL: To explore and help preserve the underwater world

ACCOMPLISHMENTS: Helped invent the Aqua-Lung diving apparatus; founded the Cousteau Society in 1974 to protect undersea habitats; educated millions through articles and television programs

LEGACY: Cousteau Society continues to pursue underwater research and conservation efforts.

A pioneer in the submarine realms that cover nearly three-fourths of the globe, Jacques Cousteau began as a French Navy diver in the 1940s. Impatient with the cumbersome hoses and other diving gear available to him, Cousteau approached engineer Émile Gagnan to help him develop a small, self-contained breathing apparatus that would allow humans to fly through the sea like fish. Thus liberated by the Aqua-Lung, Cousteau and his fellow explorers aboard his research ship, *Calypso*, spent decades probing the secrets of the seas, from underwater caves to wreck sites to sharks. When he died in 1997, he was an icon to environmentalists, underwater explorers, and all the armchair adventurers who felt that, through him, they too had "flown through the sea like fish."

EXPEDITION MEMBERS: Norman Dyhrenfurth led a 1,000-man entourage that included American mountaineers and scientists, and Sherpa porters

GOAL: To be the first Americans to summit 29,035-foot Mount Everest

ACCOMPLISHMENTS: Jim Whittaker, accompanied by Sherpa Nawang Gombu, becomes the first American on Everest; Lute Jerstad, Barry Bishop, William F. Unsoeld, and Thomas F. Hornbein follow; latter two become first to traverse a major Himalaya peak.

American Everest Expedition

"Really tired. Everything dragging.

Would love to lie on a beach somewhere and

not freeze or gasp for breath."

—AN EXPEDITION MEMBER'S
JOURNAL

It's 1963 and America is deep in the space race with Russia. But some earthbound Americans are hoping to attain new heights for the nation as well. In that spring, a U.S. team is on the slopes of mighty Everest, trying to rectify America's poor showing in mountaineering. On May 1, one of them, "Big Jim" Whittaker, along with Sherpa Nawang Gombu, gains the 29,035-foot summit. Three weeks later, four more of the Americans make it. Two—Willi Unsoeld and Tom Hornbein—have climbed the until then unconquered and unforgiving West Ridge and come down the far side of Everest. Their feat—the first traverse of a major Himalaya peak—has put Americans firmly on the world-mountaineering map. Still, the expedition suffers tragedy. Climber John Breitenbach dies in an ice fall.

Whether climbing the West Ridge (left) or slogging up the Western Cwm (far left), oxygen and working equipment (below) were essential to the expedition's success. Two members, including the Society's Barry Bishop (top left), were evacuated for treatment of frostbite.

"This jumbled mass of shattered, tortured ice
is like a prehistoric monster,
ever groaning, ever shifting, ever threatening."

—Norman G. Dyhrenfurth
Expedition Leader

Neil Merton Judd at Pueblo Bonito

Judd worked for several years excavating the jewel of Chaco Canyon, Pueblo Bonito (above and right), gaining insights into the Bonitan culture from potsherds, skeletons, and other remains (far right).

OCCUPATION: Archaeologist

PERSONAL GOALS: To understand the prehistory of the American Southwest

ACCOMPLISHMENTS: Led excavations in Chaco Canyon, including excavation of the 800-room Pueblo Bonito; staff member of the Smithsonian's Museum of Natural History (1911–1949)

LEGACY: Focused scholarly attention on the rich archaeological ground of the American Southwest

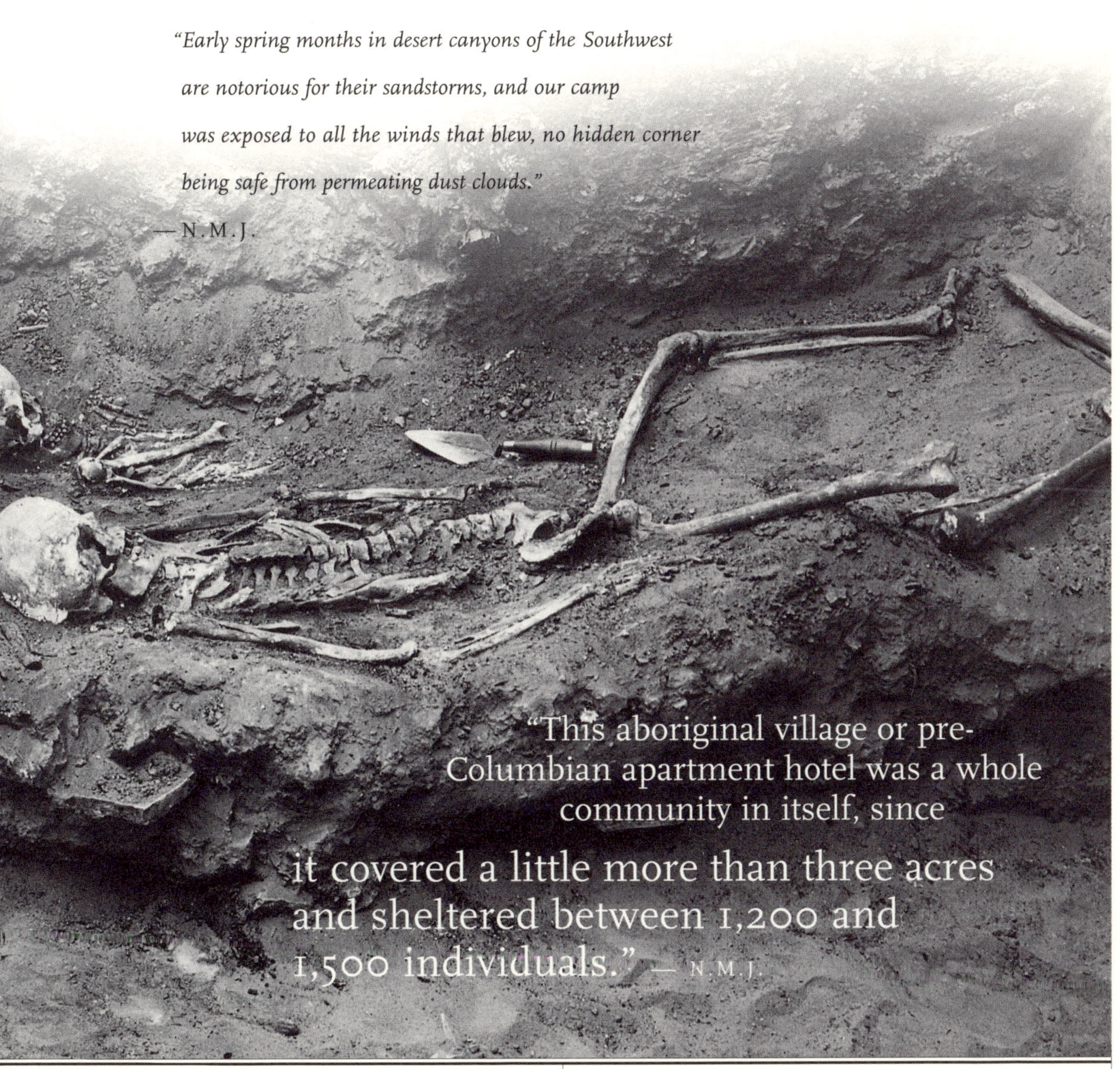

Neil Merton Judd began his romance with the arid canyon country of the Four Corners during his college days in Utah. Even after joining the staff of the Smithsonian Institution, Judd returned to the slickrock country whenever he could escape his duties. His finest moments as an archaeologist came at Pueblo Bonito—the "beautiful village"—in northwestern New Mexico's Chaco Canyon. Funded by the National Geographic Society, he spent seven seasons there, uncovering a colossal 800-room, semicircular ruin that he called a "pre-Columbian apartment hotel." The largest ever made in the American Southwest, Pueblo Bonito revealed the lost world of the Bonitans who inhabited the beautiful village more than a thousand years ago.

"Below, the shadow of our machine

"The aëroplane is the nearest thing to animate life that man has created.

In the air...it becomes animate and is capable not only of primary guidance and control,

but actually of expressing a pilot's temperament."

— R.S.

EXPEDITION MEMBERS: Sir Ross Smith (pilot), Keith Smith (navigator),
W. H. Shiers and J. M. Bennett (mechanics)

GOAL: To win the Great London-to-Australia Air Derby

ACCOMPLISHMENTS: Won derby with 27-day flight, proved commercial
feasibility of an air route between the two locations

AFTERMATH: Ross and Keith Smith knighted; Ross dies two years later
in test-flight crash.

First Vickers-Vimy Flight

pursued us, skipping from crest to crest,
jumping gulfs and ridges like a
bewitched phantom."

*Flying over four continents, the Vickers-Vimy
skirted the Italian Alps (far left), touched
down near Egypt's pyramids, crossed Java
(left), and made a tour of Australia (above).*

"Aëroplane" flight was still in its infancy when the Australian government announced the "Great London-to-Australia Air Derby." The prize: 10,000 pounds to the first to make the flight in 30 days. Unable to resist the challenge, former World War I fighter pilot Ross Smith recruited his brother Keith and two mechanics to race with him, then had a Vickers-Vimy bomber outfitted with two 360-horsepower engines. On November 12, 1919, they were off, their "great flying machine" sailing along at almost 80 miles an hour. Crammed into open cockpits on the biplane, the four men traveled light, packing only a toothbrush a piece. On December 10, 27 days after taking off, they landed in Darwin—the new heroes of the air.

— OCCUPATION: Primatologist

— PERSONAL GOALS: To observe, protect, and even befriend the endangered mountain gorillas of central Africa

— ACCOMPLISHMENTS: Contributed groundbreaking studies on gorilla behavior and raised world awareness of their fragile situation

— LEGACY: Continued awareness by environmentalists of the need to protect the Virunga gorillas, threatened even more now by civil strife

Dian Fossey

Occupational therapist Dian Fossey seemed an unlikely choice for a gorilla field researcher, but archaeologist Louis Leakey chose her anyway. Dian had met Leakey on a trip through Africa in 1963. Three years later, Leakey asked if she would give up her quiet life in Kentucky and move to the remote rain forests of the Virunga Mountains—gorilla habitat. And so began a 20-year passion that ended in death. Living in a camp in the midst of mountain gorilla terrain, Fossey learned to ape the animals' behavior and befriend them, producing groundbreaking studies. But her aggressive attempts to protect her endangered friends from poachers isolated her and ended violently. She was found dead in her cabin, with her skull crushed, in December 1985.

"Peanut seemed to ponder accepting my hand....
Finally he came a step closer and, extending his own
hand, gently touched his fingers to mine.

To the best of my knowledge
this is the first time
a wild gorilla has ever
come so close to
'holding hands' with
a human being."

— D.F.

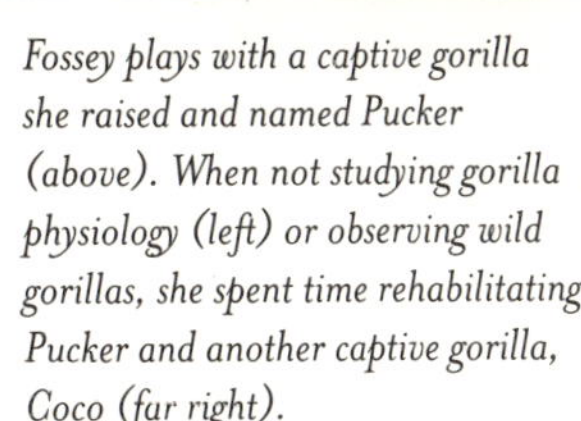

Fossey plays with a captive gorilla she raised and named Pucker (above). When not studying gorilla physiology (left) or observing wild gorillas, she spent time rehabilitating Pucker and another captive gorilla, Coco (far right).

OCCUPATION: Cartographer and museum director

PERSONAL GOALS: To excel as a mountaineer and to map the world's most rugged settings

ACCOMPLISHMENTS: Pioneered aerial mapping techniques and mapped major geologic sites, led first ascent of Alaska's 12,728-foot Mount Crillon, pioneered a new route on Mount McKinley, served as director of Boston Museum of Science (1939-1980)

"As our slow but rugged old plane
circled up out of the valley,
our eyes scanned the glowering crests
of a range of rocky peaks.
For all time—until that day—
they had concealed the secrets
of what lay in the heart
of the St. Elias Mountains."

— B.W.

As a teenager Bradford Washburn was already climbing the Alps. By the time he was at Harvard, he had made his mark on mountaineering, leading six other members of the Harvard Mountaineering Club to the 12,728-foot summit of Alaska's daunting Mount Crillon. Before the climb, he surveyed and mapped the mountain by plane. It was the beginning of a long career in mountaineering, aerial mapping, and reporting on his exploits in NATIONAL GEOGRAPHIC, *Life*, and *Look*. Often teaming with his wife, Barbara, Washburn produced maps of Mount McKinley, the Grand Canyon, and Everest. Still consumed by a madness for mapping mountains, Washburn, longtime head of Boston's Museum of Science, announced the new height of Mount Everest (29,035 feet) in November 1999.

Bradford Washburn

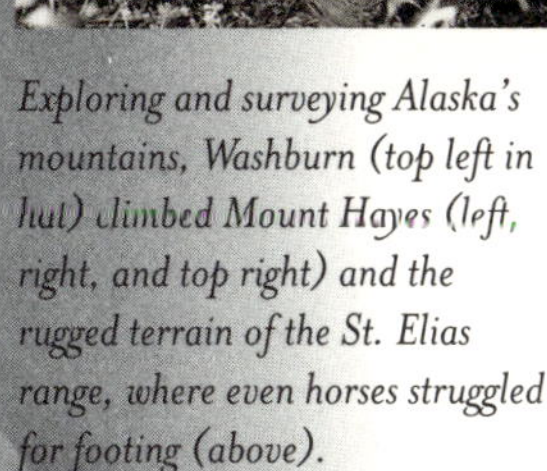

Exploring and surveying Alaska's mountains, Washburn (top left in hut) climbed Mount Hayes (left, right, and top right) and the rugged terrain of the St. Elias range, where even horses struggled for footing (above).

Charles Lindbergh

"I was astonished at the effect
my successful landing in France
had on the nations of the world.
To me, it was like a match
lighting a bonfire."

— C.L.

OCCUPATION: Aviator

PERSONAL GOAL: To advance both commercial and military aviation

ACCOMPLISHMENTS: Made the first nonstop solo transatlantic flight in 1927; flew throughout the North Atlantic with his wife, Anne Morrow Lindbergh in 1933; won the 1954 Pulitzer Prize for his book *The Spirit of St. Louis*; received a Congressional Medal of Honor

LEGACY: Became an international hero and a pioneer in the development of commercial aviation

After flying across the Atlantic, Lindbergh toured the U.S. and Latin America in the Spirit of St. Louis (above and left). Later, he and his wife, Anne Morrow Lindbergh, flew throughout the North Atlantic (top).

The "Lone Eagle," the world christened him in 1927 after his solo, nonstop flight from New York to Paris. The 25-year-old former barnstormer, wing walker, and mail pilot had flown his Ryan monoplane, the *Spirit of Saint Louis,* into aviation history, making the flight in 33 hours and 29 minutes. The press couldn't get enough of the all-American aviator, particularly after he married Anne Morrow and the two piloted themselves to countries around the globe. But tragedy struck in 1932, when the couple's two-year-old son was kidnapped, and they took refuge from the press in Europe. Though Lindbergh had a controversial relationship with the Germans during the 1930s, he threw himself into the Allied war effort, flying 50 combat missions over the Pacific.

The world's largest nonprofit scientific and educational organization, the National Geographic Society was founded in 1888 "for the increase and diffusion of geographic knowledge." Since then it has supported scientific exploration and spread information to its more than nine million members worldwide.

The National Geographic Society educates and inspires millions every day through magazines, books, television programs, videos, maps and atlases, research grants, the National Geography Bee, teacher workshops, and innovative classroom materials.

The Society is supported through membership dues and income from the sale of its educational products. Members receive NATIONAL GEOGRAPHIC magazine—the Society's official journal—discounts on Society products, and other benefits.

For more information about the National Geographic Society and its educational programs and publications, please call 1-800-NGS-LINE (647-5463), or write to the following address:

National Geographic Society
1145 17th Street N.W.
Washington, D.C. 20036-4688 U.S.A.

Visit the Society's Web site at www.nationalgeographic.com.

Melanie Doherty Design

Printed in Italy by
Poligrafiche Bolis S.p.A.

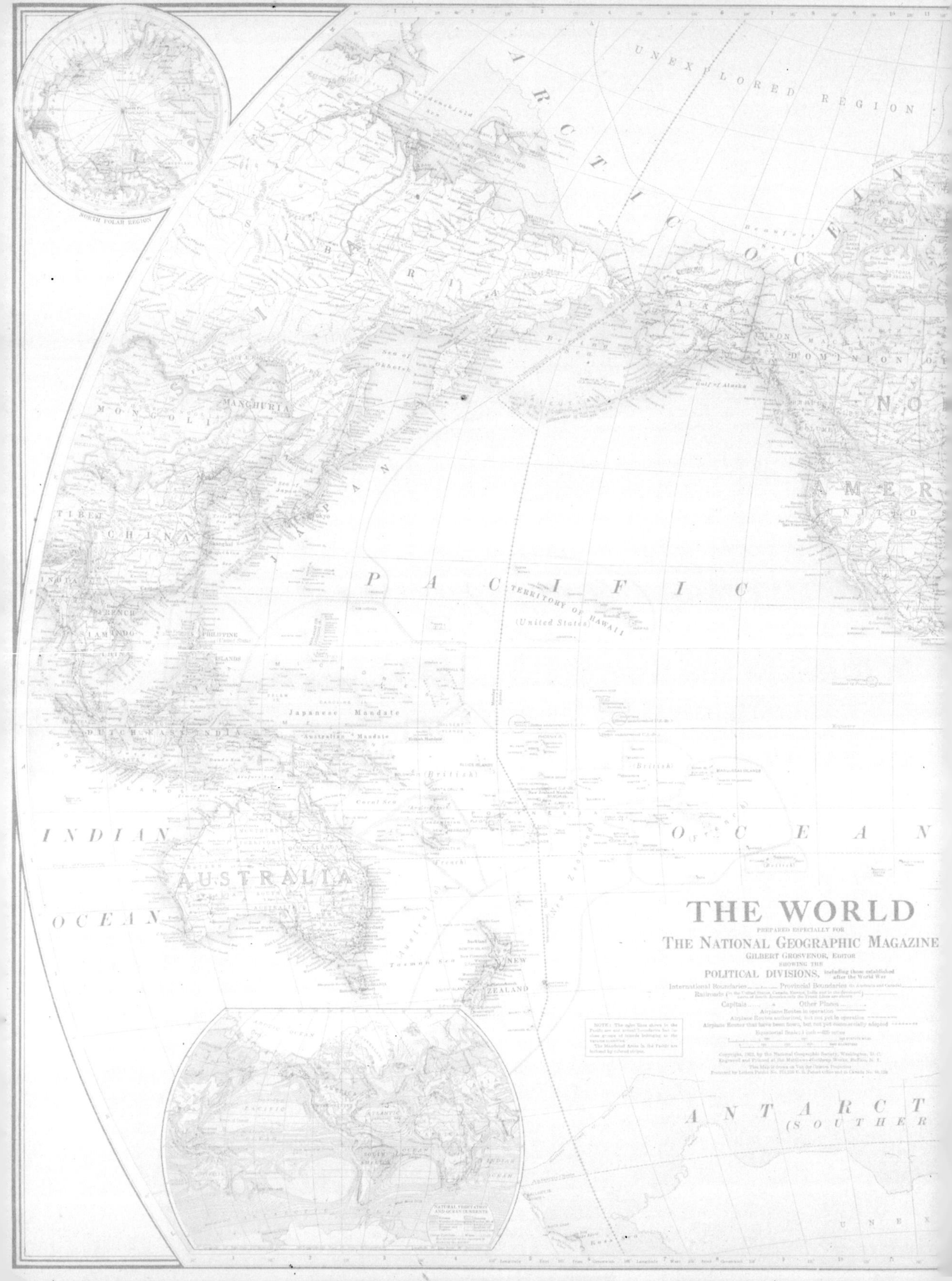

THE WORLD
PREPARED ESPECIALLY FOR
THE NATIONAL GEOGRAPHIC MAGAZINE
GILBERT GROSVENOR, EDITOR
SHOWING THE
POLITICAL DIVISIONS, including those established after the World War
International Boundaries
Provincial Boundaries (in Australia and Canada)
Railroads (in the United States, Canada, Europe, India and in the developed parts of South America only the Trunk Lines are shown)
Capitals
Other Places
Airplane Routes in operation
Airplane Routes authorized, but not yet in operation
Airplane Routes that have been flown, but not yet commercially adopted
Equatorial Scale: 1 inch = 625 miles
Copyright, 1922, by the National Geographic Society, Washington, D. C.
Engraved and Printed at the Matthews-Northrup Works, Buffalo, N. Y.
This Map is drawn on Van der Grinten Projection
Protected by Letters Patent No. 751,226 U. S. Patent Office and in Canada No. 86,126
NORTH POLAR REGION
NATURAL VEGETATION AND OCEAN CURRENTS
ARCTIC OCEAN
UNEXPLORED REGION
SIBERIA
MONGOLIA
MANCHURIA
TIBET
CHINA
INDIA
FRENCH INDO CHINA
SIAM
PHILIPPINE ISLANDS
DUTCH EAST INDIES
Sea of Japan
Sea of Okhotsk
Bering Sea
ALASKA
DOMINION OF
NORTH AMERICA
UNITED
Gulf of Alaska
PACIFIC
OCEAN
TERRITORY OF HAWAII
(United States)
Japanese Mandate
Australian Mandate
New Zealand Mandate
Coral Sea
Tasman Sea
AUSTRALIA
NEW ZEALAND
INDIAN OCEAN
ANTARCTIC
(SOUTHERN